## Mental Illnesses and Disorders

# AUTISM SPECTRUM DISORDERS

## Delayed Speech • Limited Eye Contact • Repetitive Movements • Poor Conversation Skills

H. W. Poole

MEDIA ENHANCED BOOKS
AV2 BY WEIGL™
ADDED VALUE • AUDIO VISUAL

www.av2books.com

AV² provides enriched content that supplements and complements this book. Weigl's AV² books strive to create inspired learning and engage young minds in a total learning experience.

## Your AV² Media Enhanced books come alive with...

**Audio**
Listen to sections of the book read aloud.

**Key Words**
Study vocabulary, and complete a matching word activity.

**Video**
Watch informative video clips.

**Quizzes**
Test your knowledge.

**Embedded Weblinks**
Gain additional information for research.

**Slide Show**
View images and captions, and prepare a presentation.

**Try This!**
Complete activities and hands-on experiments.

**... and much, much more!**

Go to **www.av2books.com**, and enter this book's unique code.

## BOOK CODE

### AVA77839

**AV² by Weigl** brings you media enhanced books that support active learning.

Published by AV² by Weigl
350 5th Avenue, 59th Floor
New York, NY 10118
Website: www.av2books.com

Library of Congress Control Number: 2018941347

ISBN 978-1-4896-8083-9 (hardcover)
ISBN 978-1-4896-8084-6 (softcover)
ISBN 978-1-4896-8085-3 (multi-user eBook)

Printed in Brainerd, Minnesota, United States
1 2 3 4 5 6 7 8 9 0   22 21 20 19 18

072018
120817

DEC 1 0 2019

Project Coordinator: Heather Kissock   Designer: Ana María Vidal

Every reasonable effort has been made to trace ownership and to obtain permission to reprint copyright material. The publisher would be pleased to have any errors or omissions brought to its attention so that they may be corrected in subsequent printings.

Weigl acknowledges Newscom, iStock, Shutterstock, and Alamy as its primary image suppliers for this title.

First published by Mason Crest in 2016.

# Contents

# Understanding Autism Spectrum Disorders

T racy's birth was a dream come true for her parents. She was a happy baby, and everything seemed normal at first. Soon after Tracy turned one, though, her mom started to notice that Tracy was different from other children her age. Other babies were cuddly, giving kisses and hugs to their moms. They were constantly exploring by crawling, touching things, and putting things in their mouths. They even tried to talk by babbling.

Doctors can run tests for autism on children as young as 18 months.

Tracy was not like that. She did not want to be held. She did not make eye contact. Tracy would stay on one part of the carpet, uninterested in other people. Sometimes, she would rock back and forth for long periods of time. Tracy's mom told the doctor that Tracy behaved like her mom was invisible or not in the room. The doctor examined Tracy and gave her parents the difficult news. More tests were needed, but it was very likely that Tracy had autism.

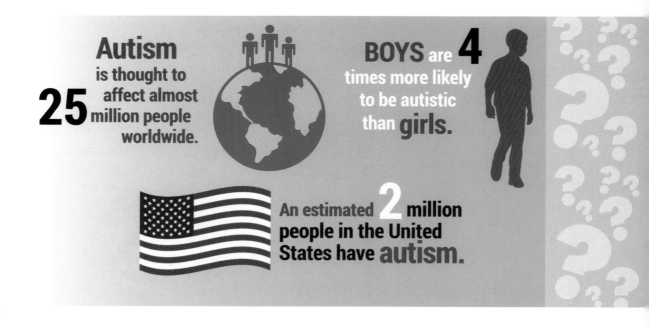

**Autism** is thought to affect almost **25** million people worldwide.

**BOYS** are **4** times more likely to be autistic than **girls**.

An estimated **2** million people in the United States have **autism**.

Children with autism may find it difficult to play with other children, preferring to play alone.

## Defining Autism

Autism is a disorder that affects two important parts of human development, communication and **socialization**. In other words, it affects how a person interacts with others. Autism can also affect how a person learns and how his or her imagination works.

The word "autism" comes from the ancient Greek word "*autos*," which means "self." The disorder was defined by Dr. Leo Kanner. In 1943, Kanner wrote a paper in which he described the symptoms that today are called autism. Before that time, children with autism were often considered to be just slow, strange, or even "crazy."

## The Spectrum

Autism has a wide range of impacts on different people. Some need a lot of help. The disorder may be so severe that the person cannot speak at all. Then there are many people with autism who grow up to have regular lives, with jobs, hobbies, and friends. It might not even be apparent that someone has autism. Autism's official name is autism **spectrum** disorder (ASD). The word "spectrum" indicates that people with autism can vary greatly from one another.

# The Autism Spectrum

Doctors describe autism in three categories, based on how much treatment individuals require. These categories are: requiring very substantial support, requiring substantial support, and requiring support. However, many people still describe themselves or their relatives by using different categories. These include autism, childhood disintegrative disorder (CDD), Asperger's syndrome, and **pervasive** development disorder, not otherwise specified (PDD-NOS).

| | Autism | Childhood Disintegrative Disorder (CDD)/ Regressive Autism | Asperger's Syndrome | Pervasive Development Disorder, Not Otherwise Specified (PDD-NOS) |
|---|---|---|---|---|
| **Symptoms may include** | • Delay in learning to talk<br>• Lack of eye contact<br>• Dislike of being touched or hugged | • Losing expressive language skills<br>• Becoming clumsy<br>• Losing interest in playing | • Being socially isolated<br>• Repetitive behavior<br>• Being physically clumsy or awkward | • Difficulty understanding language<br>• Intense dislike of changes in routine<br>• Uneven development of mental and physical skills |
| **Age at which symptoms can occur** | • 1 to 3 years old | • 2 to 10 years old | • Repetitive or narrow interests are usually clear by age six, but other symptoms occur as early as 30 months of age. | • PDD-NOS is milder than autism, and symptoms are generally recognized at a later age, sometimes not until individuals are in their teens. |
| **Treatment** | • Early intervention<br>• Individualized education plans<br>• Behavioral therapy | • Sensory enrichment therapy<br>• Behavioral therapy<br>• Antipsychotic medication where aggressive behavior presents | • Social skills training<br>• Physical therapy<br>• Behavioral therapy | • Conversation also involving stimulus such as comic strips<br>• Individualized education plans<br>• Behavioral therapy |

## Asperger's Syndrome

In 1944, an Austrian doctor named Hans Asperger noticed that a few children in his practice had very similar symptoms. They had normal or even high intelligence, but they were socially isolated. They were unable to relate to other children and had a hard time making regular conversation. These patients were both physically and socially clumsy.

Dr. Asperger wrote about these patients, describing their problems as a "personality disorder." It was many years before his work was noticed. Although Dr. Asperger did not name the syndrome after himself, when his writings were translated into English, his name became forever associated with the disorder. Asperger's syndrome used to be viewed as separate from autism. Over time, however, doctors realized that the two disorders are actually related.

## Autism and the *DSM-5*

When treating people with mental disorders, doctors refer to a guide called the *Diagnostic and Statistical Manual of Mental Disorders* (*DSM*). This manual is revised frequently to make sure that it reflects current ideas about mental illness. It has been revised five times so far. The latest edition, *DSM-5*, was published in 2013.

In earlier editions of the *DSM*, a number of disorders, including Asperger's syndrome, were considered to be separate but related disorders. Each of these was part of a larger category called pervasive developmental disorders. However, the *DSM-5* treats all those conditions as simply points on the broader autism spectrum. The older terms are still common in daily life, however. People may speak about someone who has Asperger's syndrome, for example.

Today, Asperger's syndrome is not considered to be a separate diagnosis from ASD. Some people call it "high-functioning autism." This term refers to the fact that people with Asperger's can achieve a great deal despite their disorder.

People that used to be identified with Asperger's tend to be very bright, but they can also be very limited in their interests. They often **obsess** over one particular thing. Sometimes people with Asperger's are described as "little professors" because they are so eager to share what they know. Someone with Asperger's might know absolutely everything there is to know about trains, for example. On the other hand, he may not notice or care whether you are interested in hearing about it.

People with Asperger's sometimes have trouble getting along with others. They also have huge gifts to offer, thanks to their high intelligence and intense focus. As the scientist and autism advocate Temple Grandin said in 2013, "If we got rid of ... autism, well, you wouldn't even have any computers. You wouldn't have any electricity. Who do you think made the first stone spear? It wasn't the social yakety-yaks around the campfire, that's for sure." Many of our great geniuses, especially in scientific and technical fields, may have had Asperger's.

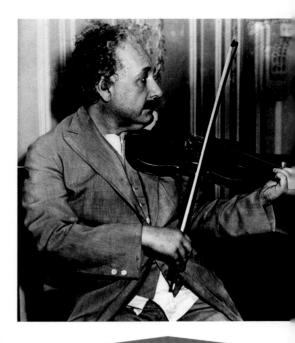

The German-born scientist Albert Einstein may have had ASD. He was highly intelligent, but he took a long time to learn to talk and had problems with learning at school.

## Take a Deeper Look

A lot has been written about geniuses of history and whether or not they had autism spectrum disorder. Not everyone agrees, but some historians have argued that Archimedes, Charles Lindbergh, Albert Einstein, and Emily Dickinson may have been on the autistic spectrum. Read a biography of one of these people. Do you agree with the opinion that the person may have had ASD? Why or why not?

# Chapter ② Major Symptoms of ASD

If you have a broken arm, it will be obvious to any doctor. If you have chicken pox, you will know it. Autism is not like that. In certain people, the symptoms are so severe that there is no doubt, of course, but for most people, things are not so obvious.

A lot of the symptoms are **subjective**. One symptom is **inflexibility**, but what seems like inflexibility to one person might seem like harmless stubbornness to someone else. Sometimes it can be difficult to tell the difference between a symptom and a personality trait. Usually, something is a symptom when it creates big challenges in the person's life. Autism symptoms can make life very difficult, both for the person with the disorder and for that person's families, friends, and teachers.

ASD symptoms also vary a lot among different people. That is why the word "spectrum" is used for autism. No two people with ASD are completely alike. However, a few symptoms are shared by a great many people with ASD.

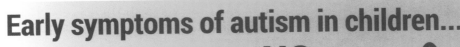
ASD expresses itself differently in different people. It is impossible to know what is going on in people's minds just by looking at them.

# Early symptoms of autism in children...

NO **single words by age 16 months**

NO **babbling or pointing by 12 months**

24 NO **two-word phrases by 24 months**

## Right Words at the Right Time

Although every person is unique, all humans follow the same general pattern of growth. For example, most babies can recognize their own names by the time they are seven months old. Some babies might do that a little earlier, and some a little later. Seven months is about the expected moment, though. In the same way, most one-year-olds can say at least a word or two, and three-year-olds can speak sentences of a few words.

One of the most important warning signs of ASD is language delay. That is the term doctors use when a child does not meet the general timeline of development. Delayed speech does not definitely mean that a child has ASD. However, it is a sign that there might be a problem. The good news is studies have shown that many children with language delay can catch up if the problem is addressed early.

Nonverbal cues can signal a person's interest or disinterest in something.

## It Is All Over Your Face

When playing a card game, an opponent's face can reveal a lot. When a card is drawn from the deck, the expression on the player's face might reveal whether it is a good card or not. Card players call this "a tell." It is an **involuntary** expression or gesture that tells what the person is thinking. This idea of the "tell" is not just for cards. People rely on "tells" all the time. Sometimes they are called social **cues** or nonverbal communication. Facial expressions, gestures, and tones of voice are all ways people tell each other things without using words.

Most people do not even think about nonverbal communication. They respond to it without even noticing. What seems obvious to them is not always obvious to people with ASD.

People with ASD often do not recognize the cues that are a natural part of daily conversation. They have to consciously learn how to recognize facial expressions. When they do, people with ASD can practice responding to social cues in useful ways.

## I Feel For You

Did you ever ask a friend, "Are you okay?" Maybe the friend shrugged sadly and said, "I'm fine." Which did you believe more, the word "fine" or the sad shrug? You probably knew that the shrug was more honest than the word. Nonverbal communication is very useful for expressing feelings. In fact, it is often better than words. For people with autism, though, these emotional cues are not at all clear.

A delay in language and social skills can mean that children with ASD have difficulty making and keeping friends.

## Other Symptoms of Autism

A significant delay in learning to talk, difficulty understanding and using facial expressions, inflexibility, and extreme reactions to certain things are all classic symptoms of autism. There are other symptoms, too. Having just one or two of these symptoms does not mean a person has autism. Also, not every person with autism has every symptom. The disorder can look different from person to person.

- an unwillingness or inability to make eye contact
- a dislike of being touched or hugged
- difficulty with regular, back-and-forth conversations
- difficulty expressing **empathy**
- repetitive movements, such as rocking back and forth
- repeating words or sounds

People with autism have trouble recognizing the emotional expressions of others. That does not mean that they are "unfeeling." It is more that their brains do not catch all the emotional signals that most people catch. For people with autism, it can seem like everyone else "talks" in an unspoken and mysterious code.

## System Overload

Although people with autism tend to miss a lot of social cues, they do notice a whole lot of other things. Another classic symptom of autism is **hypersensitivity**. Many people can find a tag in the back of a shirt annoying. For people with autism, though, sensations like that tag are not just annoying. They can be so sensitive that they might get very upset. They might find it impossible to concentrate on anything except the uncomfortable shirt. Different people can be sensitive to different things. Some people with autism are disturbed by particular sounds, tastes, textures, or smells.

## Old Habits

All people have certain things that they want to be a certain way. They know the "best" route to school, for example. They have a favorite chair they always sit in. They have a favorite pair of socks they always wear on specific days. Habits and rituals make everyone feel safe in an uncertain world.

Sometimes, though, things do not go to plan. There is construction on the road to school. Someone else is sitting in the favorite chair. The favorite socks are in the washing machine. That is okay, though. They might not like it, but most people adjust.

The repetition of everyday tasks, such as tying shoelaces in a certain way, can be very important for people with ASD.

People with autism often cannot adjust, or they can only adjust with great difficulty. What most people would see as a minor annoyance can be incredibly upsetting to people with autism. For example, a child with autism might insist that the family drive the same way to school every day, no matter what. He might be terribly upset at school if there is a substitute teacher he was not expecting. Repetition and familiarity are very important to many people with ASD.

## Autism and Play

When young animals play, they are practicing skills, such as hunting and chasing. When children play, they practice important skills with their games, too. Play helps children practice how to wait their turn, how to compromise, and how to handle disappointment when they lose. Play is a very important part of human development.

One problem is that some children with ASD do not understand how to play. Their minds tend to be much more **literal** than most. A child who sees an empty box might imagine that it is a rocket ship, or a castle, robot, or getaway car. A child with ASD is more likely to simply see a box. Instead of playing pretend with stuffed animals, a child with ASD is more likely to line up the animals in alphabetical order.

This creates several problems. First, it is harder for children with ASD to understand what other children are doing or talking about when they play imaginatively. Second, children with ASD do not get to practice all those skills that others learn through play. Therapy for children with ASD often involves helping their imaginations stretch and grow. With help and practice, kids with ASD can be ready to ride that rocket ship, too.

**D**r. Leo Kanner was the first to describe the condition now called autism spectrum disorder (ASD). Dr. Kanner also made another important contribution to the understanding of autism. In his 1943 paper, Dr. Kanner described the condition as "**innate**." That is, he suspected that people with autism were born with the condition. He noticed that autistic traits seemed to be more common in some families than in others. This observation led him to consider possible **genetic** causes.

Doctors no longer believe that parents are the cause of ASD.

Today, describing a mental condition as innate is not very controversial. When Dr. Kanner was writing, though, most people believed that mental problems were caused by experiences in childhood. In fact, doctors used to believe that autism was caused by parents who did not love their children. This idea even had a nickname. "Refrigerator mothers," or those who were cold to their children, were blamed for causing the disorder.

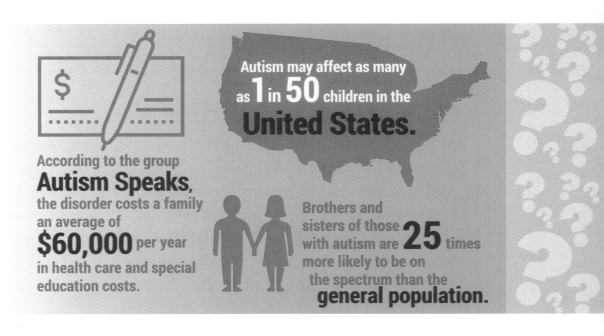

According to the group **Autism Speaks**, the disorder costs a family an average of **$60,000** per year in health care and special education costs.

Autism may affect as many as **1** in **50** children in the **United States.**

Brothers and sisters of those with autism are **25** times more likely to be on the spectrum than the **general population.**

## Genetics and Autism

Today, doctors know that Dr. Kanner's idea that autism is innate is correct. One or several genetic **mutations** play at least some role in ASD.

Studies have found that if one identical twin has ASD, the other twin will also have the disorder at least 70 percent of the time. This is strong evidence for a genetic link. Yet, it also means that 30 percent of the time, one twin has ASD while the other does not. So whatever the genetic link might be, it is not a simple one.

Studying identical twins can help researchers discover more about the genetic link in ASD.

Even if both twins have ASD, they can have different symptoms. For example, one may have more challenges with language skills. The other twin might have more challenges with emotional skills. ASD can look different not only from one person to another, but also from one twin to another.

## Race, Ethnicity, and ASD

ASD has been found in children of every **ethnic** background. Caucasian children are more likely to be **diagnosed** with ASD than children of other races, though. Experts do not yet know whether Caucasian children are truly more at risk of ASD. In many parts of the United States, Caucasian people tend to have better access to health care. A lack of access might affect experts' understanding of how many children of other races have ASD. That is, it is possible other children do get ASD at the same rates as Caucasians, but they are not diagnosed at the same rates.

There are several reasons why this might be true. First, brain development is extremely complex. Experts are only beginning to understand how and why brains develop the way they do. It is possible that identical twins could have the same genetic mutation, but the mutation could express itself in different ways.

It is also likely that ASD has a secondary cause. That is, maybe it is not genetics alone, but rather genetics plus some other factor. A person's genetics might make him or her more at risk for ASD, but it might be something else that **triggers** the disorder. In twins with ASD, one twin might have been more strongly influenced by that trigger than the other.

## Environment and Autism

When you think about the word "environment," you might think about air or water pollution. In fact, **toxins** from the environment may be a trigger for ASD. Autism cases are known to cluster around particular geographical areas. This has led some researchers to wonder if something in the environment, such as a toxin, causes autism rates to rise in that community. So far, no specific toxin has been proven to cause ASD.

When doctors talk about "environmental" causes of ASD, they do not just mean air, water, and so on. They also mean the whole context in which a baby develops. For example, the children of parents who are aged 40 and older are slightly more likely to develop ASD. Folic acid, a substance in food that is vital to brain development, might have a role to play. Pregnant women who are low in folic acid may be more likely to have autistic children. Being born premature at a very low weight might also be associated with developing ASD later on. Research continues on all these environmental factors.

Green, leafy vegetables such as kale are good sources of folic acid. Women are advised to increase their intake of folic acid when they are pregnant.

## Vaccines and Autism

To sum up, there is a lot experts still do not know about the causes of ASD. This is very frustrating, both for doctors and for families. People want answers. Parents of very young children want to know if there is anything they can do to protect their babies. Unfortunately, widespread fear can cause people to jump to conclusions. People want answers so badly that they are tempted to believe anything that "seems right." This has definitely been the case when it comes to the issue of autism and vaccines.

In 1998, a study was published in a British medical journal called the *Lancet*. The study seemed to suggest a connection between a common childhood vaccine and symptoms of ASD. The study was very small and involved only 12 children, but it led to a panic.

## The First Vaccine

Smallpox is a deadly **virus** that has killed hundreds of millions of people. In fact, some historians have argued that smallpox killed more people than every other virus combined. In the 1790s, an English doctor named Edward Jenner figured out that by exposing someone to a tiny amount of a less harmful version of the virus, that person would become **immune** to the deadlier version. At first, people mocked Jenner's idea. In time, though, the wisdom of vaccinating people became clear. Jenner's idea has saved an uncountable number of human lives. Thanks to vaccination, smallpox was wiped out in the late 1970s.

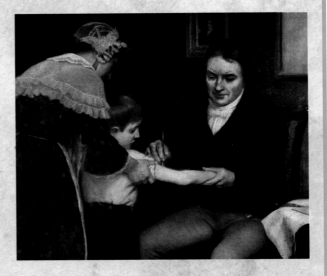

The symptoms of ASD tend to appear when children are around three years old. This also is when children get a lot of vaccinations. So the idea that the two events were connected "seemed right" to a lot of parents. Before long, books and websites were echoing the claims of the study. Self-proclaimed experts went on television to warn parents about the "danger" of vaccines. Congress even held hearings on the topic.

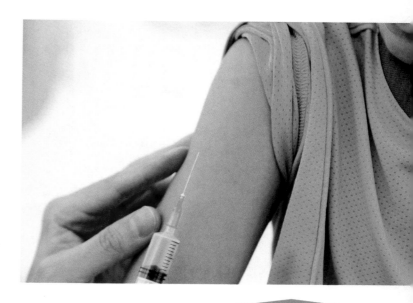

Meanwhile, no other studies were able to recreate the results of that 1998 *Lancet* study. In time, it became clear why. The *Lancet* study was a fraud. It claimed that the children had developed ASD symptoms within days of vaccination, but that turned out to be untrue. The main author of the study had misrepresented his results. The *Lancet* **retracted** the study in 2011, saying that it is "utterly clear, without any ambiguity at all, that the statements in the paper were utterly false."

There is no scientific evidence that vaccines are involved in causing ASD. The group Autism Speaks says that it "strongly encourage(s) parents to have their children vaccinated for protection against serious disease."

The Centers for Disease Control and Prevention recommend vaccinating against a large number of diseases. These include diptheria, tetanus, whooping cough, measles, mumps, rubella, hepatitis A and B, and chicken pox.

## Take a Deeper Look

Find out more about Edward Jenner and his smallpox vaccine. Why did people react so badly to the idea at first? How has Jenner's work been improved upon by modern scientists? What other diseases have been brought under control with vaccination?

**A**lthough there is no cure for autism, there are lots of things people can do to manage their autism. People who have severe ASD may always need extra help. The majority of people with ASD can learn to handle the challenges of their disorder and have independent lives.

## Early Detection

It is very important for people with ASD to get help as soon as possible. Early treatment leads to better outcomes. When parents suspect that their child may have a problem, it is important to find a team of professionals who are experienced with diagnosing autism.

ASD experts favor specific tools, such as the Autism Diagnostic Observation Schedule and the Autism Diagnostic Interview. Doctors need special training to be able to use these tools. These extra methods of evaluation help doctors understand the specifics of a particular child's problems. They also help prevent **misdiagnosis**.

The Autism Diagnostic Observation Schedule examines patients' responses and behavior in four main areas. These are communication, imagination, social skills, and play skills.

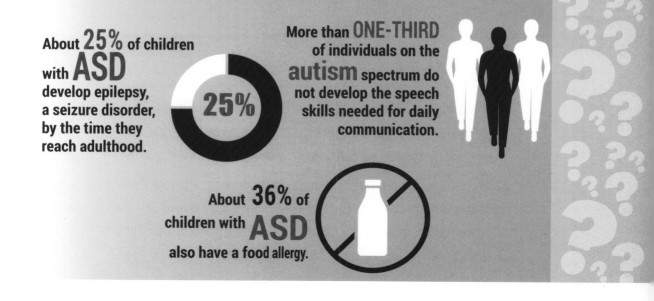

About **25%** of children with **ASD** develop epilepsy, a seizure disorder, by the time they reach adulthood.

**25%**

More than **ONE-THIRD** of individuals on the **autism** spectrum do not develop the speech skills needed for daily communication.

About **36%** of children with **ASD** also have a food allergy.

Once children are diagnosed, they are then sent for treatment. Every person with ASD is different, so every person's **therapy** must be different. Experts tailor programs to the specific needs of the individual.

## Extra Challenges

When it comes to ASD, the concept of **comorbidity** is important. It means that people can have more than one disorder at a time. Several disorders are very common for people who also have ASD. Often, managing autism begins with managing these other troubles first.

Sleep problems can lead to daytime sleepiness, learning problems, and issues with behavior, such as aggression.

SLEEP PROBLEMS. As many as 80 percent of children with ASD may have at least some trouble sleeping at some point. Sometimes children with ASD have trouble with their circadian rhythm. That is the internal system that tells people when to wake up and when to sleep. Keeping a regular schedule of sleep times and waking times can do a lot to help people sleep. Specially designed programs can help kids with ASD get the most out of their education. Sometimes physical problems keep children with ASD awake. Doctors can help find possible solutions to sleep problems.

## Plan for Problems

People with ASD have trouble adjusting to change. Routines in their lives help them manage. This could mean anything from predictable schedules to predictable menus. All these routines help people with ASD lower their anxiety.

Life is not always predictable, though. At some point, a person might be unable to follow some part of his or her routine. It is a good idea to talk through what happens next. It may also be useful to have some plans in mind for what happens if a loved one with ASD is upset by sudden change.

**STOMACH PROBLEMS. Gastrointestinal** problems are very common among people with ASD. Sometimes these problems result from the autism. For example, someone might be very sensitive to the taste, smell, or texture of particular foods. This might lead that person to have a limited diet, which can cause digestion problems. Doctors call this maladaptive behavior. The ASD symptoms lead a person to make choices that are bad for her physical health. Improving the diet can help ease these problems. Getting more fiber by eating more fruits, vegetables, and whole grains is one way to improve diet.

Some people believe that ASD is not caused by stomach problems, but that it can be made worse by gastrointestinal problems. A recent trend involves managing ASD through diet. One popular diet is called GFCF, which stands for "gluten free, casein free." Gluten is found in wheat and many other products, and casein is found in dairy. Someone on a GFCF diet must not eat bread, pasta, cookies, milk, ice cream, or cheese. She also has to be careful about taking vitamins, which often contain gluten.

A number of studies have been conducted on GFCF diets and autism. So far, there is no conclusive proof that the diet works. Some studies have found no improvement at all, while a few others have found evidence that certain children with ASD might benefit. Children who have ASD and gastrointestinal problems gain the most from dietary changes.

Some parents report that their children's autism got a lot better with the GFCF diet. Some experts have wondered if a healthier diet overall, with less sugar, fat, and processed foods, might be the real source of the improvement. Everyone can agree, though, that there needs to be more study of GFCF and the role of diet in general.

Some experts have suggested that toxins in the intestines may trigger autism or make it worse in some children.

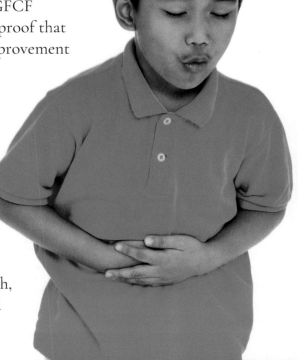

## Important Diet Advice

It is important for parents to work closely with their pediatrician and other treatment providers when making dietary changes. When dairy is taken out of the diet, for example, a major source of calcium is taken out. Calcium is hugely important for children because it helps bones grow strong. Young people on a GFCF diet need to be very careful to replace all the nutrients they lose. For example, broccoli and kale are two good sources of calcium. These green vegetables also contain fiber, which is also important if whole grains are avoided.

**ANXIETY AND DEPRESSION.** It is not hard to imagine why many people with ASD also have anxiety. Many of the symptoms, such as not being able to understand social cues, would cause anxiety in most people. If you had trouble understanding the things people say, the world might seem like a very threatening place.

Children with ASD may feel frustrated in school, which can lead to depression.

Depression is also a common problem for people with ASD. People with ASD sometimes have trouble making friends, but that does not mean they do not want friends. ASD can make people feel very isolated and lonely. Children with ASD may feel that they will never be "normal" the way other children are. It is also possible that some of these psychiatric symptoms are caused by some of the brain differences in people with autism.

The good news is there is lots of help and hope for people with depression and anxiety, whether they have ASD or not. Talking to a doctor or counselor is a good start. Sometimes a low dosage of medication can make a huge difference for people with ASD.

# If You Have ASD

The challenges of ASD, such as hypersensitivity to noise, inflexibility, or not being able to read people's facial expressions, are not easy to live with. However, with time and patience, it is possible to manage the disorder.

## Early Intervention

All states have programs for children who show delays in development from infancy until age three.

## Individualized Education Plans (IEPs)

Parents can work with schools to create an IEP. It can involve special attention in class, extra teaching, and monitoring of progress.

## Specially Trained Teachers

Some teachers are specially trained in ASD. These teachers are able to work out the best approach for each individual.

## Behaviorial Therapy

Therapists can help children improve their communication, language, learning, and coping skills, and can offer counseling.

## Family Therapy

Some families can get therapy to learn strategies to help their child manage symptoms of his or her ASD.

## Applied Behavior Analysis (ABA)

ABA is especially good at helping children with autism learn language and social skills. The programs can be very intensive.

# ASD over Time

**A**SD is a modern disease, and not much was written about it before the 1900s. The study and treatment of ASD became important in the last 100 years. Today, doctors recognize it is a serious problem for children.

## 1910

Swiss doctor Eugen Bleuler used the word "autism" to describe a group of patients he was treating for the mental disease schizophrenia. These patients were especially withdrawn and self-absorbed.

## 1943

Austrian-American doctor Dr. Leo Kanner used the term "autism" in a paper he wrote about 11 children. He described these children as having "early infantile autism."

## 1977

U.S. researchers Dr. Susan Folstein and Professor Michael Ritter conducted research on twins with autism. They found that autism is largely caused by genetics and biological differences in brain development.

Each person with ASD is different and needs to be evaluated by a professional to determine the best treatment.

## 1987

UCLA psychologist Dr. Ole Ivar Lovaas published the first study on the effect of intensive behavioral therapy on children with autism. It showed how therapy can help children manage their autism, giving new hope to parents.

## 1988

The movie *Rain Man* was released. It starred Dustin Hoffman as an autistic man who has a photographic memory and can calculate huge numbers in his head. Few children on the autism spectrum have these kinds of skills.

## 2016

Taylor Duncan, a man on the autism spectrum, set up the Alternative Baseball Organization. Its aim is to teach skills and to provide a social outlet for children and adults with ASD through sport.

# Quiz

**1** What key parts of human development are affected in people with ASD?

**2** Why is the word "spectrum" used in the term "autism spectrum disorder"?

**3** What are the characteristics of someone with Asperger's syndrome?

**4** What is hypersensitivity?

**5** What important contribution did Dr. Leo Kanner make to the study of ASD?

**6** Do vaccinations cause ASD?

**7** Do doctors believe that ASD can be cured?

**8** What methods do doctors use to find out whether someone has ASD?

**9** What are three ways that doctors in the United States treat ASD today?

**10** What are other problems that people with ASD may commonly have?

**ANSWERS**

**1** Communication and socialization. **2** Because people with autism can vary greatly from one another **3** High intelligence and intense focus. **4** Being too sensitive to things such as noise **5** He recognized that ASD is an innate problem. **6** No **7** No. It can be managed but not cured. **8** They use the Autism Diagnostic Observation Schedule and interview. **9** Early intervention, individualized education plans, and therapy **10** Problems with sleep, the stomach, anxiety, and depression

# Key Words

**comorbidity:** two or more illnesses appearing at the same time

**cues:** signals

**diagnosed:** to have identified a problem

**empathy:** understanding someone else's situation and feelings

**ethnic:** relating to races or large groups of people who have the same customs and origin

**gastrointestinal:** relating to the stomach and digestion

**genetic:** relating to heredity

**hypersensitivity:** being too sensitive

**immune:** not affected by something

**inflexibility:** unwillingness or inability to adapt or change

**innate:** existing from the beginning

**involuntary:** automatic

**literal:** describing someone who understands the world in a concrete way, without much imagination

**misdiagnosis:** an incorrect identification of a problem

**mutations:** in genetics, changes in the structure of a gene

**obsess:** to focus completely on a particular feeling or object

**pervasive:** widespread

**retracted:** to have taken back

**socialization:** the way a person behaves with others

**spectrum:** a range

**subjective:** not based on observation, affected by personal feelings

**therapy:** treatment of a problem, either with medicine or by talking with a therapist

**toxins:** poisons

**triggers:** causes something to happen

**virus:** an extremely small particle that causes a disease

# Index

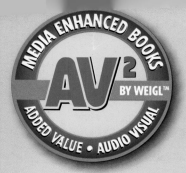

# Log on to www.av2books.com

AV² by Weigl brings you media enhanced books that support active learning. Go to www.av2books.com, and enter the special code found on page 2 of this book. You will gain access to enriched and enhanced content that supplements and complements this book. Content includes video, audio, weblinks, quizzes, a slide show, and activities.

## AV² Online Navigation

**Audio**
Listen to sections the book read alo...

**Book Pages**
AV² pages directly correspond to pages in the book.

**Video**
Watch informative video clips.

**Key Words**
Study vocabulary, and complete a matching word activity.

**Embedded Weblinks**
Gain additional information for research.

**Quizzes**
Test your knowledge.

**Slide Show**
View images and captions, and prepare a presentation.

**Try This!**
Complete activities and hands-on experiments.

AV² was built to bridge the gap between print and digital. We encourage you to tell us what you like and what you want to see in the future.

## Sign up to be an AV² Ambassador at www.av2books.com/ambassador.

# LIK

★ VOLUME THREE ★
## HULK NO MORE

★ C O L O R S ★
### JASON KEITH
### AND GURU eFX
VS.
### DAN BROWN &
### CHRIS SOTOMAYOR
(ROUND 4)
### DAN BROWN
(ROUND 5)

★ ON THE UNDERCARD ★
### WRITER AUDREY LOEB
AND
### ARTIST & LETTERER CHRIS GIARRUSSO

"HULK BEACH"
"HULK MAMA"
"HULK CHEF"
"HULK DOG"
"HULK DRIVING"
"HULK BURGER"

★ ASSISTANT EDITOR ★
**NATHAN COSBY**

★ EDITOR ★
**MARK PANICCIA**

---

★ COLLECTION EDITOR ★
**JENNIFER GRÜNWALD**

★ ASSISTANT EDITORS ★
**ALEX STARBUCK**
**& JOHN DENNING**

★ EDITOR, SPECIAL PROJECTS ★
**MARK D. BEAZLEY**

★ SENIOR EDITOR, SPECIAL PROJECTS ★
**JEFF YOUNGQUIST**

★ SENIOR VICE PRESIDENT OF SALES ★
**DAVID GABRIEL**

★ BOOK DESIGN ★
**JOHN ROSHELL**
**OF COMICRAFT**

---

★ EDITOR IN CHIEF ★
**JOE QUESADA**

★ PUBLISHER ★
**DAN BUCKLEY**

★ EXECUTIVE PRODUCER ★
**ALAN FINE**

OL. 3: HULK NO MORE. Contains material originally published in magazine form as HULK #10-13 and INCREDIBLE HULK
rst printing 2009. Hardcover ISBN# 978-0-7851-3983-6. Softcover ISBN# 978-0-7851-4052-8. Published by MARVEL
HING, INC., a subsidiary of MARVEL ENTERTAINMENT, INC. OFFICE OF PUBLICATION: 417 5th Avenue, New York, NY 10016.


7 6 5 4 3 2 1

# ROUND ★ ONE

## LOVE AND DEATH

ONCE UPON A TIME.
IN THE HEART OF AN ATOM.
THERE LIVED A WORLD...

...WHERE THE HULK
WAS A HERO. AND
VERY MUCH IN LOVE.

TODAY, I HAVE
ASKED THE
PRINCESS JARELLA
TO MARRY ME
AND --

-- I HAVE
ACCEPTED!

HULK!
HULK!
HULK!
HULK!

HULK!

SO MUCH
HAPPINESS.

MY BRAIN.
THE HULK'S
POWER.

BEING A MAN
OF SCIENCE, IT'S
STILL HARD TO BELIEVE
YOUR WIZARDS COULD
DO IT --

HUSH,
MY LOVE. NO
MORE TALK OF
SCIENCE --

-- JUST THAT
WE HAVE FOUND
EACH OTHER DESPITE
BEING UNIVERSES
APART IS MAGIC
ENOUGH FOR --

WHAT IS IT?
WHAT'S
HAPPENING?!

I DON'T
KNOW -- !

JARELLA. YOU
ARE NEEDED...
ELSEWHERE.

YOU **ARE** ALL FROM DIFFERENT YEARS. SOME HAVING NEVER MET...**YET.**

I MADE MY DEAL WITH THE HULK **IN THE PRESENT.** HE ALONE GOT TO PICK HIS WARRIORS --

-- BUT I WOULD SELECT FROM **WHEN** YOU CAME.

EACH OF YOU SUFFERED A GREAT LOSS AT THESE TEMPORAL POINTS.

EACH OF YOU WERE AT YOUR MOST VULNERABLE.

YOU WOULD EACH **DIE** TO SAVE YOUR RESPECTIVE LOVED ONE.

THAT'S OF GREAT VALUE IN THE GAME.

WHAT GAME? HOW DO I KNOW YOU CAN RETURN THE LADY DORMA TO MY SIDE?

BECAUSE, AVENGING SON, SINCE THE DAWN OF TIME, AN ELDER HAS NEVER BROKEN A **TRUE** PROMISE.

NOW, IT IS TIME TO MEET MY BROTHER --

**THE COLLECTOR!**

WELL PLAYED, BROTHER. YOU'VE PUT TOGETHER A FORMIDABLE GROUP --

-- TOO BAD I HAD THE SAME NOTION AND BEGAN WITH **THE OTHER HULK** TO COLLECT **MY** CHAMPIONS.

WHAT OTHER HULK?

ATLANTIS.
I DON'T WANT TO FIGHT YOU.
AFTER THE BEATING YOU GAVE ME LAST TIME, I DON'T WANT TO FIGHT YOU EITHER...
TRAPPED IN A WORLD

THEY NEVER MADE

IT MATTERS LITTLE.

MY BROTHER IS DEAD.

THEN BRING HIM BACK TO LIFE AS YOU DID THE REST OF US.
AND THEN RETURN THE WOMEN WE LOVE AS PROMISED.

WHEN AN ELDER DIES... RESURRECTION IS NEARLY IMPOSSIBLE. I KNOW FROM FIRST-HAND EXPERIENCE.

AS TO THE BARGAIN REGARDING YOUR WOMEN, THAT WAS WITH MY BROTHER.
I MADE NO SUCH ARRANGEMENT.

WHITE HAIR BRING JARELLA HERE.

I HAVE LOST MY BROTHER. DO NOT ORDER ME --

BRING JARELLA HERE OR HULK WILL BREAK YOU.

AS YOU WISH. YOU WILL SEE HER AS SHE IS... AS SHE ALWAYS WILL BE...

HULK... BE CAREFUL WHAT YOU WISH FOR...

# ROUND ★ FOUR

# SEEING RED

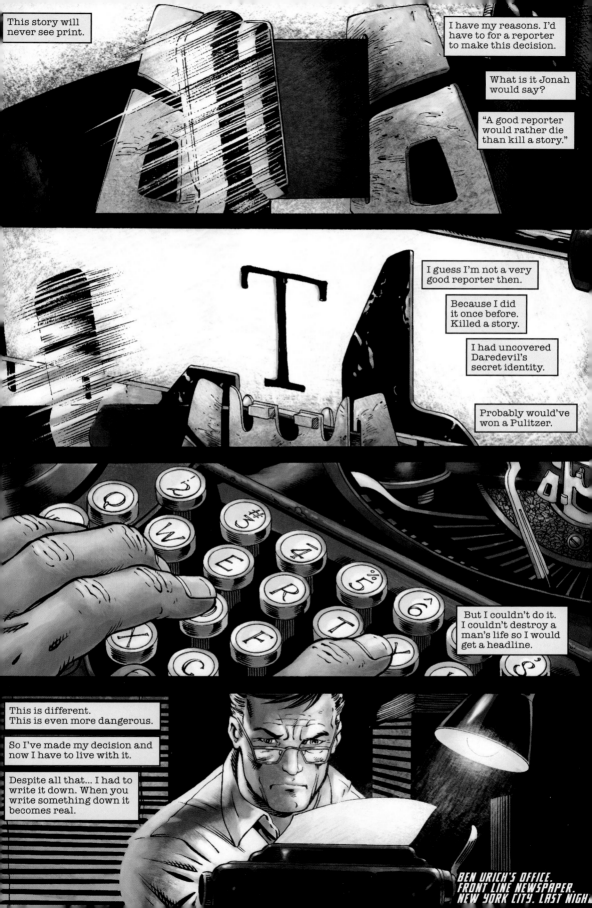

This story will never see print.

I have my reasons. I'd have to for a reporter to make this decision.

What is it Jonah would say?

"A good reporter would rather die than kill a story."

I guess I'm not a very good reporter then.

Because I did it once before. Killed a story.

I had uncovered Daredevil's secret identity.

Probably would've won a Pulitzer.

But I couldn't do it. I couldn't destroy a man's life so I would get a headline.

This is different. This is even more dangerous.

So I've made my decision and now I have to live with it.

Despite all that... I had to write it down. When you write something down it becomes real.

BEN URICH'S OFFICE. FRONT LINE NEWSPAPER. NEW YORK CITY. LAST NIGH

The story actually began with an ending. Several months ago. Here in New York.

THE HULK had declared war on the world.

THE INCREDIBLE
HULK
SEEING
RED

The war was over.

The Hulk was defeated. That's what mattered.

GET THE LEAD OUT, PEOPLE.

I WANT *BANNER* GONE FROM THIS CITY *NOW*.

Banner was handed over to S.H.I.E.L.D.

There would be no trial. It was Guantanamo all over again.

After all that had happened, if you couldn't call the Hulk a terrorist...

And as far as anyone knows...

...that was the end of the story....

Three nights ago.
I got a phone call.
To go to a garage off 21st.

Alone.

It's times like that I wish I hadn't quit smoking.

HELLO...?

DID YOU CHANGE CABS?

WHAT? YES. *SIX* TIMES. JUST LIKE YOU TOLD ME TO. I ALMOST GOT LOST MYSELF.

COULDN'T WE HAVE DONE THIS OVER THE PHONE?

PHONES AREN'T SAFE.

WHAT'S THIS ALL ABOUT?

THE HULK.

OR MORE SPECIFICALLY. THE *HULKS.*

...

THERE'S MORE THAN *ONE* HULK?

UNBELIEVABLE.

YES. THERE ARE *TWO* HULKS.

ONE GREEN.

THE OTHER *RED.*

AND...?

WHO IS THE RED HULK?

THAT'S WHAT YOU'LL HAVE TO FIND OUT.

THIS SEEMS MORE OF A *NATIONAL STORY.* I USUALLY COVER THE NEW YORK --

-- PEOPLE SAY YOU CAN BE TRUSTED. THAT YOU'LL KEEP YOUR WORD.

AREN'T YOU *SHE-HULK?* GO SMASH HIM OR WHATEVER YOU DO.

I TRIED... HE'S...TOO STRONG. BUT IF YOU COULD *EXPOSE* HIM. GET *THE TRUTH* OUT THERE...

PEOPLE ARE WATCHING ME.

WHO? *THE GOVERNMENT?*

I'VE BEEN ASKING TOO MANY QUESTIONS.

IF...I DO THIS, I NEED TO KNOW WHAT YOU KNOW. YOU'RE SO PARANOID YOU'VE GOTTEN *ME* PARANOID.

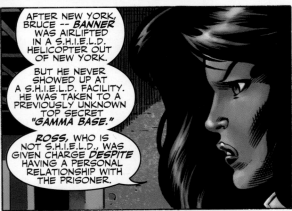

AFTER NEW YORK, BRUCE -- *BANNER* WAS AIRLIFTED IN A S.H.I.E.L.D. HELICOPTER OUT OF NEW YORK.

BUT HE NEVER SHOWED UP AT A S.H.I.E.L.D. FACILITY. HE WAS TAKEN TO A PREVIOUSLY UNKNOWN TOP SECRET *"GAMMA BASE."*

*ROSS,* WHO IS NOT S.H.I.E.L.D., WAS GIVEN CHARGE *DESPITE* HAVING A PERSONAL RELATIONSHIP WITH THE PRISONER.

THE RED HULK MURDERED THE ABOMINATION. STOLE FILES FROM S.H.I.E.L.D. AND THE BAXTER BUILDING. WRECKED A HELICARRIER AND ALL OF THAT HAS REMAINED *CLASSIFIED?!*

THEN... *HOW* DO YOU KNOW ABOUT ANY OF THIS?

BE AT J.F.K. TOMORROW NIGHT. U.S. AIR. FLIGHT 659. TO LAS VEGAS.

SOMEONE WILL MEET US. SOMEONE WE CAN TRUST.

WHO...?

BRING A *PHOTOGRAPHER.* YOU'RE GOING TO NEED PHYSICAL EVIDENCE.

WAIT A SECOND. WHY LAS VEGAS?

DID YOU CHANGE CABS?

YES! I CHANGED --

HELLO...?

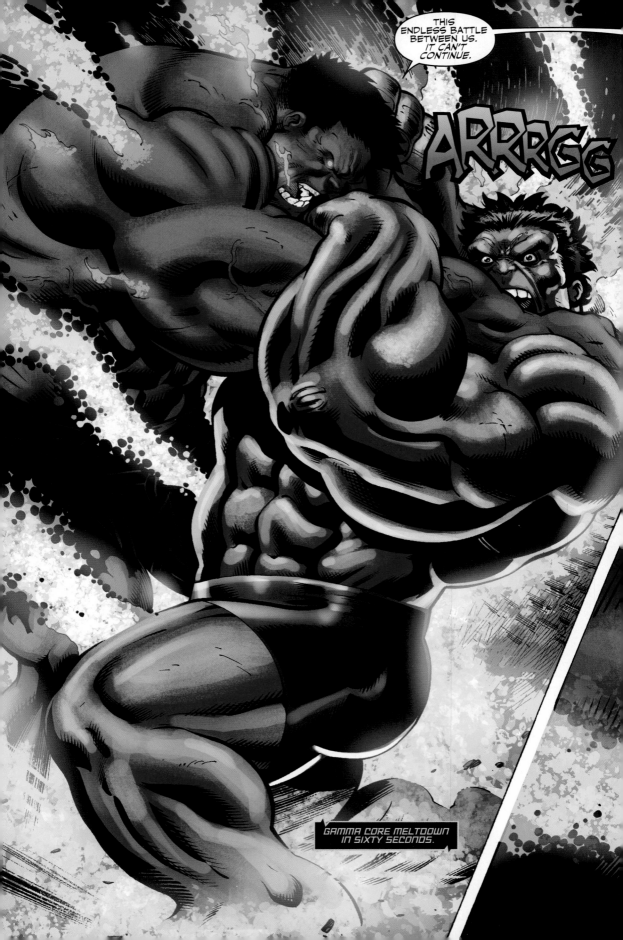

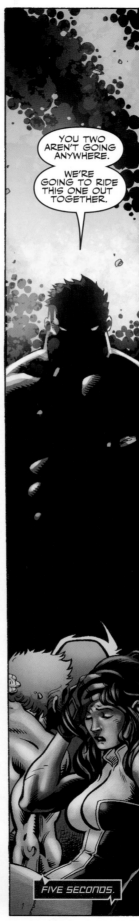

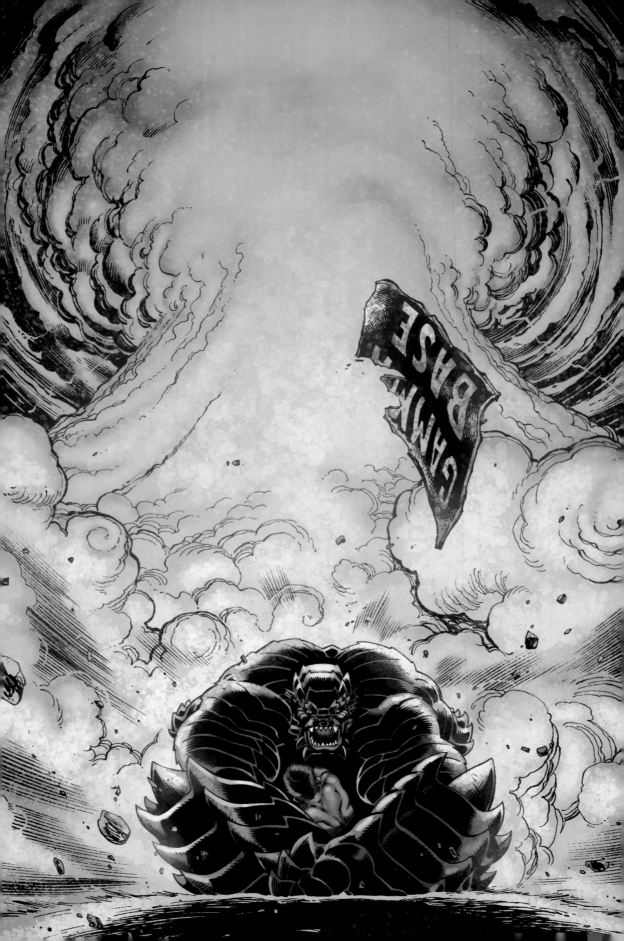

But there wasn't going to be a story.

URICH.

YOU. YOU SURVIVED.

DID YOU REALLY THINK THAT IF A GUTLESS MILKSOP LIKE YOU COULD GET OUT, I WOULDN'T?

AND WHAT ABOUT *JENNIFER*... SHE-HULK? IS SHE ALL RIGHT?

I DIDN'T COME HERE TO TALK ABOUT *SHE-HULK*.

WELL, IF YOU THINK YOU CAN INTIMIDATE ME, GET IN LINE. I'VE BEEN THREATENED BY DANGEROUS MEN ALL MY LIFE.

WHO? *THE KINGPIN?* DON'T MAKE ME LAUGH.

DO YOU KNOW HOW MANY BUILDINGS WERE KNOCKED DOWN THE LAST TIME THE HULK WENT ON A RAMPAGE?

TWENTY? TEN? LET'S SAY IT WAS ONLY *ONE*.

WHAT IF IT WERE THE BUILDING WHERE EVERYONE AT *FRONT LINE* WORKS?

DURING A STAFF MEETING. *THE ENTIRE STAFF MEETING*.

ROBBIE ROBERTSON.

PETER PARKER.

MAYBE YOU CALLED IN SICK THAT DAY.

YOU COULD WRITE ALL ABOUT IT.

# ROUND ★ FIVE

# HULK NO MORE

They say when you go through the death of someone you love there are five stages of relief.

I meant.

Grief.

Odd that I would make that mistake.

Grief.

Relief.

I suppose that's the kind of conversation I could have with Leonard...

...If Samson were the kind of man I could ever trust again.

For the longest time I've lived with a nightmare.

That the monster inside me would come out.

That it would never end.

A monster that I, alone, created.

Causing destruction in every aspect of my life. Love. Family.

Everything.

And now that I've woken up from the nightmare...

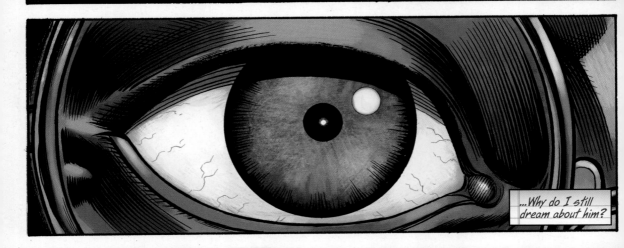

...Why do I still dream about him?

Is it that I trapped him inside of me for so long that I'm not ready to deal with his death?

All I wanted was to be rid of him...

...Shouldn't saying good-bye be the easiest thing in the world?

I know in my heart that I have to move on with my life...

...except...

I don't believe THE HULK is dead...

HOW--HOW DID YOU DO THAT? ADAPT TO THE ENVIRONMENT LIKE THAT?

ALWAYS THE SCIENTIST, HUH, BRUCE?

I'M NOT SURE, REALLY.

SOMETHING ELSE M.O.D.O.K. DID TO ME. OR I COULD ALWAYS DO ONCE I BECAME...A-BOMB.

AND I JUST DIDN'T KNOW HOW.

PRETTY FRICKIN' COOL.

I GUESS NOW WE KNOW WHAT'D HAPPEN IF AN ARMADILLO AND A CHAMELEON HAD A BABY.

A REALLY FUGLY BABY --

-- WHO'S STRONG AS ALL GET OUT!

I'M STILL AMAZED THAT YOU'VE TAKEN CONTROL OF A-BOMB'S PERSONALITY.

YOU NO LONGER REFER TO YOURSELF IN THE THIRD PERSON.

LIKE I USED TO...

"HULK AM STRONGEST THERE IS..."

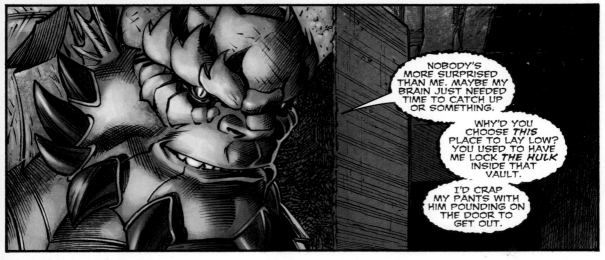

NOBODY'S MORE SURPRISED THAN ME. MAYBE MY BRAIN JUST NEEDED TIME TO CATCH UP OR SOMETHING.

WHY'D YOU CHOOSE THIS PLACE TO LAY LOW? YOU USED TO HAVE ME LOCK THE HULK INSIDE THAT VAULT.

I'D CRAP MY PANTS WITH HIM POUNDING ON THE DOOR TO GET OUT.

THINK YOU'RE A TOUGH GUY -- PUSHING AROUND GUYS WHO CAN'T DEFEND THEMSELVES, HUH?

YOU'RE MORE LIKE THE GOD OF *WHATEVER.*

NO ONE. NOT MAN. NOR BEAST. INSULTS ME AND LIVES.

THAT WILL BE THE LAST LESSON YOU LEARN IN THIS WORLD.

NOW, BANNER --

IRONIC, ISN'T IT?

WHAT IS?

I CAN'T CHANGE INTO A MONSTER.

AND YOU CAN'T CHANGE OUT OF IT.

I KINDA LIKE BEING PART OF THE "STRONGEST THERE IS" CLUB NOW.

I THINK AS YOU GET MORE USED TO IT, IT'S NOT ALL THAT IT'S CRACKED UP TO BE.

BUT YOU HAVE TO LEARN THAT FOR YOURSELF.

WHERE YOU OFF TO, BRUCE?

I JUST FIGURED... AFTER ALL THOSE YEARS THAT YOU PROTECTED ME--

--I COULD PROTECT YOU. KINDA PAYBACK, Y'KNOW.

LIKE YOU DID WITH ARES?

GO LIVE YOUR LIFE, RICK. LIKE I'VE GOT TO LIVE MINE.

TAKE CARE OF YOURSELF, DOC.

"Live my life."

It's been so long, I don't even know who Bruce Banner is anymore. All I know is...

I am not the Hulk.

3 1191 00917 4285

THE END.

# ★ EXTRAS ★

# COVER GALLERY

★ I S S U E   1 0   C O V E R S

ED McGUINNESS & GURU eFX ★

★ I S S U E   1 1   C O V E R S

ED McGUINNESS & GURU eFX ★

ISSUE 12 VARIANT COVER ★ ED McGUINNESS & GURU eFX

★ ISSUE 12 VARIANT COVER

ARTHUR ADAMS & FERRAN DELGADO ★

MARVEL 70th FRAME VARIANT COVER ★ MICHAEL GOLDEN

ISSUE 13 VARIANT COVER ★ JOHN ROMITA JR. & DEAN WHITE

★ INCREDIBLE HULK 600 VARIANT COVER

ED McGUINNESS & DAN BROWN ★

# SKETCHBOOK

NO HALOS!          NO HALOS!

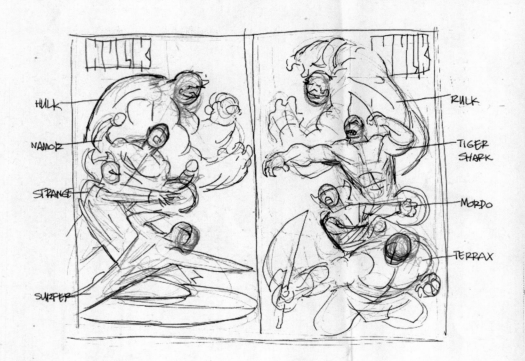

HULK

NAMOR

STRANGE

SURFER

RULK

TIGER SHARK

MORDO

TERRAX

**BONUS FEATURES**

**NATHAN COSBY** - *Editor*          **JOE QUESADA** - *Editor In Chief*          **DAN BUCKLEY** - *Publisher*

# HULK MAMA

WRITTEN BY **AUDREY LOEB**
ILLUSTRATED BY CHRIS GIARRUSSO  chrisGcomics.com

**JORDAN D. WHITE** - *Editor*        **JOE QUESADA** - *Editor In Chief*        **DAN BUCKLEY** - *Publisher*

# HULK CHEF

WRITTEN BY AUDREY LOEB
ILLUSTRATED BY CHRIS GIARRUSSO  chrisGcomics.com

**JORDAN D. WHITE** - *Editor*          **JOE QUESADA** - *Editor In Chief*          **DAN BUCKLEY** - *Publisher*

# HULK DOG

WRITTEN BY AUDREY LOEB
ILLUSTRATED BY CHRIS GIARRUSSO chrisGcomics.com

**JORDAN D. WHITE** - Editor          **JOE QUESADA** - Editor In Chief          **DAN BUCKLEY** - Publisher

# HULK DRIVING
## WRITTEN BY AUDREY LOEB
ILLUSTRATED BY CHRIS GIARRUSSO  chrisGcomics.com

**JORDAN D. WHITE** - *Editor*          **JOE QUESADA** - *Editor In Chief*          **DAN BUCKLEY** - *Publisher*

# HULKDONALD'S

WRITTEN BY AUDREY LOEB
ILLUSTRATED BY CHRIS GIARRUSSO  chrisGcomics.com

**JORDAN D. WHITE** - Editor          **JOE QUESADA** - Editor In Chief          **DAN BUCKLEY** - Publisher